First published in Great Britain 1980 by
Hamish Hamilton Childrens Books
Garden House, 57-59 Long Acre, London WC2E 9JZ

ISBN 0 241 10506 4

Printed in Italy

THE FAITHFUL BULL

Ernest Hemingway

pictures by

MICHAEL FOREMAN

HAMISH HAMILTON • London

One time there was
a bull and his name
was not Ferdinand
and he loved to fight
and he fought with
all the other bulls
of his own age,
or any age,
and he was champion.

His horns were as solid as wood and they were as sharply pointed as the quill of a porcupine. They hurt him, at the base, when he fought, and he did not care at all. His neck muscles lifted in a great lump that is called in Spanish the *morillo* and this *morillo* lifted like a hill when he was ready to fight.

He was always ready to fight and his coat was black and shining and his eyes were clear.

Anything made him want to fight and he would fight with deadly seriousness exactly as some people eat or read or go to church. Each time he fought to kill and the other bulls were not afraid of him because they came of good blood and were not afraid. But they had no wish to provoke him. Nor did they wish to fight him.

He was not a bully nor was he wicked, but he liked to fight as men might like to sing or be the King or the President.
He never thought at all. Fighting was his obligation and his duty and his joy.

He fought on the stony, high ground. He fought under the cork oak trees and he fought in the good pasture by the river.

He walked fifteen miles each day from the river to the high, stony ground and he would fight any bull that looked at him. Still he was never angry.

That is not really true, for he was angry inside himself. But he did not know why, because he could not think. He was very noble and he loved to fight.

So what happened to him? The man who owned him, if anyone can own such an animal, knew what a great bull he was and still he was worried because this bull cost him so much money by fighting with other bulls. Each bull was worth over one thousand dollars and after they had fought the great bull they were worth less than two hundred dollars and sometimes less than that.

So the man, who was a good man, decided that he would keep the blood of this bull in all of his stock rather than send him to the ring to be killed. So he selected him for breeding.

But
this bull was a strange bull.

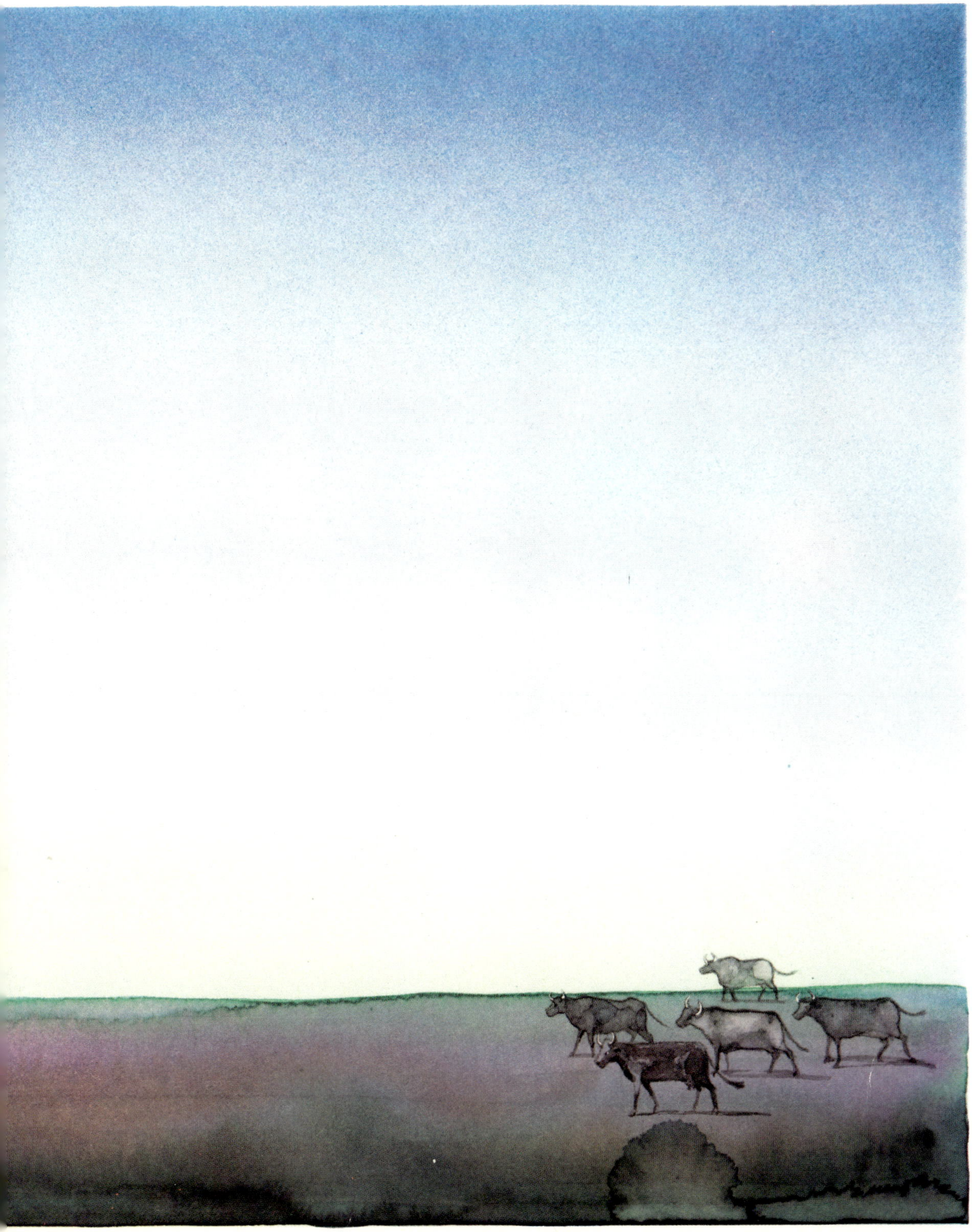

When they first turned him into the pasture with the breeding cows, he saw one who was young and beautiful and slimmer and better muscled and shinier and more lovely than all the others.

So, since he could not fight,
he fell in love with her and
he paid no attention to any of the others.

He wanted only to be with her, and the others meant nothing to him at all.

The man who owned the bull ranch hoped that the bull would change, or learn or be different than he was. But the bull was the same and he loved whom he loved and no one else.

So the man sent him away with five other bulls to be killed in the ring, and at least the bull could fight, even though he was faithful.

He fought
wonderfully and everyone admired him and the man who killed him admired him the most.

But the fighting jacket of the man who killed him and who is called the matador was wet through by the end, and his mouth was very dry.

"Que Toro mas bravo," the matador said as he handed his sword to his sword handler. He handed it with the hilt up and the blade dripping with the blood from the heart of the brave bull who no longer had any problems of any kind and was being dragged out of the ring by four horses.

"Yes he was the one the Marqués of Villamayor had to get rid of because he was
the sword handler, who knew everything said.

1,”

"Perhaps we should all be faithful" the matador said.